Metropolitan Women

ADDRESS BOOK

THE METROPOLITAN MUSEUM OF ART, NEW YORK
CHRONICLE BOOKS, SAN FRANCISCO

The works of art reproduced in this book are from
the collections of The Metropolitan Museum of Art.

Cover:
In the Studio (detail)
Alfred Stevens, Belgian, 1823–1906
Oil on canvas, 42 × 53½ in., 1888
Gift of Mrs. Charles Wrightsman, 1986 1986.339.2

Title page:
Study for "Raphael and the Fornarina"
Jean-Auguste-Dominique Ingres, French, 1780–1867
Graphite on white wove paper, 10 × 7¼ in.
Robert Lehman Collection, 1975 1975.1.646

Opposite:
At the Louvre: Mary Cassatt in the Etruscan Gallery
Edgar Degas, French, 1834–1917
Softground etching, drypoint, aquatint, and etching
10½ × 9⅛ in., 1879–80
Rogers Fund, 1919 19.29.2

Published by The Metropolitan Museum of Art, New York,
and Chronicle Books, 275 Fifth Street, San Francisco, California 94103

Produced by the Department of Special Publications,
The Metropolitan Museum of Art
Photography for Édouard Manet's
Mademoiselle V. . . in the Costume of an Espada
by Malcolm Varon, N.Y.
All other photography by
The Metropolitan Museum of Art Photograph Studio
Designed by Tina Fjotland

Distributed in Canada by Raincoast Books
8680 Cambie Street
Vancouver, B.C. V6P 6M9

ISBN 0-87099-731-9 (MMA)
ISBN 0-8118-1075-5 (Chronicle)
First Edition
10 9 8 7 6 5 4 3 2 1

Printed in Italy

Metropolitan women—sophisticated, bohemian, intrepid, demure, contemplative, industrious—appear in many guises in this elegant address book. Each divider page features two images of women, one on each side, as captured by artists through the ages. Ingres's exquisite *Portrait of the Princesse de Broglie* appears with Goya's proud *Doña Narcisa Barañana de Goicoechea*; an intricately wrought Indian miniature of women enjoying an outdoor banquet accompanies Gauguin's painting of exotic Tahitian women; and an arresting portrait of the glamorous Marlene Dietrich

is companion to a shimmering photograph of the dynamic Josephine Baker. The works of art range from paintings to drawings, photographs, tapestry, and stained glass, and are all from the rich collections of The Metropolitan Museum of Art.

Portrait of the Princesse de Broglie
Jean-Auguste-Dominique Ingres, French, 1780–1867
Oil on canvas, 47¾ × 35¾ in., 1851–53
Robert Lehman Collection, 1975   1975.1.186

A

Doña Narcisa Barañana de Goicoechea
Francisco de Goya y Lucientes, Spanish, 1746–1828
Oil on canvas, 44¼ × 30¾ in.
H. O. Havemeyer Collection
Bequest of Mrs. H. O. Havemeyer, 1929   29.100.180

Name Paula Ashley

Address 59 Candleberry St

Harvard, Ma

Telephone 1-978-456-3058

Name Abbott's Animal Hospital

Address

Telephone 508 - 853-3350

Name

Address

Telephone

Name

Address

Telephone

Name

Address

Telephone

Name

Address

Telephone

Name

Address

Telephone

Name

Address

Telephone

Name

Address

Telephone

Name	Name
Address	Address
Telephone	Telephone

Name	Name
Address	Address
Telephone	Telephone

Name	Name
Address	Address
Telephone	Telephone

Name	Name
Address	Address
Telephone	Telephone

Name	Name
Address	Address
Telephone	Telephone

Name

Address

Telephone

Name

Address

Telephone

Name

Address

Telephone

Name

Address

Telephone

Name

Address

Telephone

Name

Address

Telephone

Name

Address

Telephone

Name

Address

Telephone

Name

Address

Telephone

Name

Address

Telephone

Name

Address

Telephone

Name

Address

Telephone

Name

Address

Telephone

Name

Address

Telephone

Name

Address

Telephone

Name

Address

Telephone

Name

Address

Telephone

Name

Address

Telephone

Name

Address

Telephone

Name

Address

Telephone

L'Arlésienne: Madame Joseph-Michel Ginoux
(Marie Julien, 1848–1911)
Vincent van Gogh, Dutch, 1853–1890
Oil on canvas, 36 × 29 in., 1888
Bequest of Sam A. Lewisohn, 1951   51.112.3

Gertrude Stein
Pablo Picasso, Spanish, 1881–1973
Oil on canvas, 39⅜ × 32 in., 1906
Bequest of Gertrude Stein, 1946   47.106

Name Erica Burke
Address 23 Gorham St
Somerville, Ma. 02144
Zack 617-308-1787 -- Scott's 617-240-5916
Telephone 617-230-2815
WK- 617-267-3900

Name Benson + Woods Auto
Address
Telephone 508 - 757-8381

Name Margo Brunelli
Address 7 Fidders handing
Harwich port 02648
Telephone 508 - 430-2970

Name Burke - Ireland - Bobby
Eileen, Michael, Williams Eileen
Address
Wallace
McGeeny, Co Cork, Fire
Telephone

Name Dr. Bayon
Address Grove St
Worc, Ma.
Telephone 508 - 755-0372

Name PC Bertrands
Address 8710 Azalea court
apt 2020
Tumara, Fl. 33321
Telephone 954 - 726-6390

Name Donna Bayrouty
Address 541 Pheasant St
Worc
Telephone 508 - 752 - 7113

Name Joyce Beaudy
Address Box 1153
7 Liberty Place
East Dennis 02641
Telephone 508- 385-8860

Name Emily Bertrand
Address 300 Nathan Ellis
#6 High way
Mashpee, Ma. 02649
Telephone 954 - 501-1183

Name Pan Selita Brown
Address 6 Bobwhite Crescent
Mashpee 02649
Telephone 508 - 477-1791

Name MaryAnn Bardier
Address P.O. Box 139
Charlton Depot, Ma
01509
her Mother's 508 736-9423
Telephone 508 -248-4761

Name
Address

Telephone

Name
Address

Telephone

Name
Address

Telephone

Name
Address

Telephone

Name
Address

Telephone

Name
Address

Telephone

Name
Address

Telephone

Name
Address

Telephone

Name	Name
Address	Address
Telephone	Telephone

Name	Name
Address	Address
Telephone	Telephone

Name	Name
Address	Address
Telephone	Telephone

Name	Name
Address	Address
Telephone	Telephone

Name	Name
Address	Address
Telephone	Telephone

Name	Name
Address	Address
Telephone	Telephone
Name	Name
Address	Address
Telephone	Telephone
Name	Name
Address	Address
Telephone	Telephone
Name	Name
Address	Address
Telephone	Telephone
Name	Name
Address	Address
Telephone	Telephone

A Lady with Two Gentlemen (detail)
Tapestry from a set possibly made for Charles VII
of France, Southern Netherlands
Wool warp; wool, silk and metallic weft yarns;
entire tapestry 9 ft. 7 in. × 10 ft. 11¾ in.; 1450–55
Rogers Fund, 1909   09.137.2

Queen Kunigunde
Austrian, from the Church of St. Leonhard
in Lavanthal, Carinthia
Pot-metal glass, 38½ × 17½ in., 1340–50
The Cloisters Collection, 1965   65.96.4

Name Mary Callaghan
Address 99 Main St. unit 7
Westford, Ma. 01886
Per Heinke 978-389-4858
Telephone 978- 692-1842

Name Noreen Castle
Address Home Cottage
15010 Farnham Lane
Farnham, Surrey
Telephone GU9 8JU England

Name Stephanie Church
Address 473 Spring St
West Bridgewater, Ma
02379
wk - 781-383-2088
Telephone 508-586-3597
Cell 781-985-0066

Name Steph's Friends
Address Joanne + Bill Flanagan
781-331-0551
Debbie Keenan 860-739-
8586
Telephone

Name Andy Church
Address 1050 Main St
Weymouth, Ma. 02190

Telephone 781- 985-1029

Name Mary + John (Callaghan)
Haggarity
Address

Telephone 01-3532 / 4646916

Name Pauline Calabro
Address 16 Winter St
Waltham, Ma. 02154

Telephone 781- 899-9762

Name Sheila Callaghan
Address 96 Nesmith St
Lawrence, Ma 01841-
4448
Telephone 978- 688-0252

Name Jackie Callaghan
Address 20 Ridge Crest Terr.
West Roxbury 02132
Apt #3
Telephone 617- 323-7658

Name Church Summer Htn
Address Drive 10 - 302
Cleveland, NY. 13042
General Delivery
Telephone 315- 675-8132

Name Marjorie E. Cahn
Address 634 Walden St
Concord, Ma. 01742
Telephone 978-341-0186

Name Marjie Cahn-Cype
Address
Car Phone -cell 508-450-4446
Telephone 508-255-6626

Name Rita Callaghan
Address 70 St. Botolph St
Boston, 02116
Apt. 711
Telephone 617-267-6690

Name
Address

Telephone

Cype Name Pam + Jay Rabeuhsen
Address neighbors,

Telephone 508-436-2686

Name
Address

Telephone

Name
Address

Telephone

Name
Address

Telephone

Name
Address

Telephone

Name
Address

Telephone

Name	Name
Address	Address
Telephone	Telephone
Name	Name
Address	Address
Telephone	Telephone
Name	Name
Address	Address
Telephone	Telephone
Name	Name
Address	Address
Telephone	Telephone
Name	Name
Address	Address
Telephone	Telephone

Name

Address

Telephone

Name

Address

Telephone

Name

Address

Telephone

Name

Address

Telephone

Name

Address

Telephone

Name

Address

Telephone

Name

Address

Telephone

Name

Address

Telephone

Name

Address

Telephone

Name

Address

Telephone

Young Woman with a Water Jug
Johannes Vermeer, Dutch, 1632–1675
Oil on canvas, 18 × 16 in.
Marquand Collection
Gift of Henry G. Marquand, 1889   89.15.21

The Musician
Bartholomeus van der Helst, Dutch, 1613–1670
Oil on canvas, 54½ × 43¾ in., 1662
Purchase, 1873   73.2

Name Patti +Tim Doolittle   Name

Address 13 White Farm Rd   Address

Wingdahe, NY. 12594

Telephone 914-832-3626   Telephone

Name   Name

Address   Address

Telephone   Telephone

Name   Name

Address   Address

Telephone   Telephone

Name   Name

Address   Address

Telephone   Telephone

Name   Name

Address   Address

Telephone   Telephone

Name

Address

Telephone

Name

Address

Telephone

Name

Address

Telephone

Name

Address

Telephone

Name

Address

Telephone

Name

Address

Telephone

Name

Address

Telephone

Name

Address

Telephone

Name

Address

Telephone

Name

Address

Telephone

Name	Name
Address	Address
Telephone	Telephone

Name	Name
Address	Address
Telephone	Telephone

Name	Name
Address	Address
Telephone	Telephone

Name	Name
Address	Address
Telephone	Telephone

Name	Name
Address	Address
Telephone	Telephone

Name	Name
Address	Address
Telephone	Telephone
Name	Name
Address	Address
Telephone	Telephone
Name	Name
Address	Address
Telephone	Telephone
Name	Name
Address	Address
Telephone	Telephone
Name	Name
Address	Address
Telephone	Telephone

Lady Lilith
Dante Gabriel Rossetti, British, 1828–1882
Watercolor and gouache on paper,
20³/₁₆ × 17⁵/₁₆ in., 1867
Rogers Fund, 1908   08.162.1

The Toilet of Venus
François Boucher, French, 1703–1770
Oil on canvas, 42⅝ × 33½ in., 1751
Bequest of William K. Vanderbilt, 1920   20.155.9

Name Carol Evans
Address 256 Lull Water Dr
P.O. Box 14228
Panama City Beach, FL
32413

Telephone 850-233-1211

Name

Address

Telephone

Name

Address

Telephone

Name

Address

Telephone

Name

Address

Telephone

Name

Address

Telephone

Name

Address

Telephone

Name

Address

Telephone

Name

Address

Telephone

Name	Name
Address	Address
Telephone	Telephone
Name	Name
Address	Address
Telephone	Telephone
Name	Name
Address	Address
Telephone	Telephone
Name	Name
Address	Address
Telephone	Telephone
Name	Name
Address	Address
Telephone	Telephone

Name	Name
Address	Address
Telephone	Telephone
Name	Name
Address	Address
Telephone	Telephone
Name	Name
Address	Address
Telephone	Telephone
Name	Name
Address	Address
Telephone	Telephone
Name	Name
Address	Address
Telephone	Telephone

Name	Name
Address	Address
Telephone	Telephone
Name	Name
Address	Address
Telephone	Telephone
Name	Name
Address	Address
Telephone	Telephone
Name	Name
Address	Address
Telephone	Telephone
Name	Name
Address	Address
Telephone	Telephone

Marlene Dietrich
James Doolittle, American, active 1920s–1930s
Gelatin silver print, 16¼ × 12¹³⁄₁₆ in., ca. 1931
Ford Motor Company Collection, Gift of Ford Motor
Company and John C. Waddell, 1987   1987.1100.26

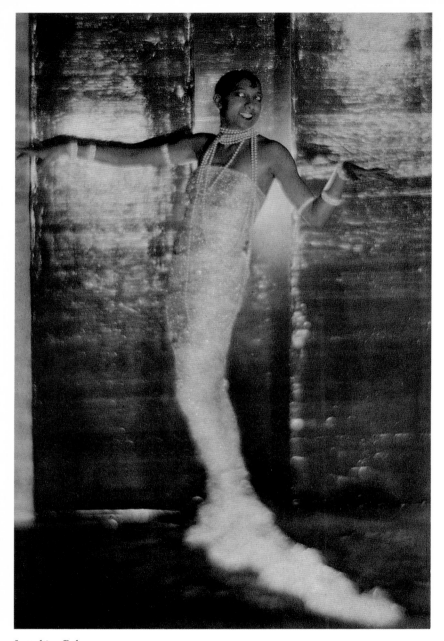

Josephine Baker
Baron Adolph de Meyer, American (b. France), 1868–1949
Gum bichromate over platinum print,
17¾ × 11⅝ in., ca. 1923
Ford Motor Company Collection, Gift of Ford Motor
Company and John C. Waddell, 1987   1987.1100.16

Name

Address

Telephone

Name

Address

Telephone

Name

Address

Telephone

Name

Address

Telephone

Name

Address

Telephone

Name

Address

Telephone

Name

Address

Telephone

Name

Address

Telephone

Name

Address

Telephone

Name

Address

Telephone

Name	Name
Address	Address
Telephone	Telephone
Name	Name
Address	Address
Telephone	Telephone
Name	Name
Address	Address
Telephone	Telephone
Name	Name
Address	Address
Telephone	Telephone
Name	Name
Address	Address
Telephone	Telephone

Name	Name
Address	Address
Telephone	Telephone
Name	Name
Address	Address
Telephone	Telephone
Name	Name
Address	Address
Telephone	Telephone
Name	Name
Address	Address
Telephone	Telephone
Name	Name
Address	Address
Telephone	Telephone

Name

Address

Telephone

Name

Address

Telephone

Name

Address

Telephone

Name

Address

Telephone

Name

Address

Telephone

Name

Address

Telephone

Name

Address

Telephone

Name

Address

Telephone

Name

Address

Telephone

Name

Address

Telephone

Woman with a Parrot
Édouard Manet, French, 1832–1883
Oil on canvas, 72⅞ × 50⅝ in., 1866
Gift of Erwin Davis, 1889   89.21.3

Madame X (Madame Pierre Gautreau)
John Singer Sargent, American, 1856–1925
Oil on canvas, 82⅛ × 43¼ in., 1884
Arthur Hoppock Hearn Fund, 1916   16.53

Name	Name
Address	Address
Telephone	Telephone
Name	Name
Address	Address
Telephone	Telephone
Name	Name
Address	Address
Telephone	Telephone
Name	Name
Address	Address
Telephone	Telephone
Name	Name
Address	Address
Telephone	Telephone

Name	Name
Address	Address
Telephone	Telephone

Name	Name
Address	Address
Telephone	Telephone

Name	Name
Address	Address
Telephone	Telephone

Name	Name
Address	Address
Telephone	Telephone

Name	Name
Address	Address
Telephone	Telephone

Name	Name
Address	Address
Telephone	Telephone

Name	Name
Address	Address
Telephone	Telephone

Name	Name
Address	Address
Telephone	Telephone

Name	Name
Address	Address
Telephone	Telephone

Name	Name
Address	Address
Telephone	Telephone

Name

Address

Telephone

Name

Address

Telephone

Name

Address

Telephone

Name

Address

Telephone

Name

Address

Telephone

Name

Address

Telephone

Name

Address

Telephone

Name

Address

Telephone

Name

Address

Telephone

Name

Address

Telephone

Portrait of a Man and a Woman at a Casement
Fra Filippo Lippi, Italian (Florentine), ca. 1406–1469
Tempera on wood, 25¼ × 16½ in.
Marquand Collection
Gift of Henry G. Marquand, 1889   89.15.19

Portrait of a Young Woman
Lorenzo di Credi (Lorenzo d'Andrea d'Oderigo),
Italian (Florentine), 1459/60−1537
Oil on wood, 23⅛ × 15¾ in.
Bequest of Richard De Wolfe Brixey, 1943   43.86.5

Name

Address

Telephone

Name

Address

Telephone

Name

Address

Telephone

Name

Address

Telephone

Name

Address

Telephone

Name

Address

Telephone

Name

Address

Telephone

Name

Address

Telephone

Name

Address

Telephone

Name

Address

Telephone

Name
Address

Telephone

Name
Address

Telephone

Name
Address

Telephone

Name
Address

Telephone

Name
Address

Telephone

Name
Address

Telephone

Name
Address

Telephone

Name
Address

Telephone

Name
Address

Telephone

Name
Address

Telephone

Name	Name
Address	Address
Telephone	Telephone
Name	Name
Address	Address
Telephone	Telephone
Name	Name
Address	Address
Telephone	Telephone
Name	Name
Address	Address
Telephone	Telephone
Name	Name
Address	Address
Telephone	Telephone

Name	Name
Address	Address
Telephone	Telephone
Name	Name
Address	Address
Telephone	Telephone
Name	Name
Address	Address
Telephone	Telephone
Name	Name
Address	Address
Telephone	Telephone
Name	Name
Address	Address
Telephone	Telephone

Woman with a Pink
Rembrandt van Rijn, Dutch, 1606–1669
Oil on canvas, 36¼ × 29⅜ in.
Bequest of Benjamin Altman, 1913   14.40.622

Portrait of a Woman, Probably Susanna Lunden
(née Fourment, 1599–1628)
Peter Paul Rubens, Flemish, 1577–1640
Oil on wood, 30¼ × 23⅝ in.
Gift of Mr. and Mrs. Charles Wrightsman, 1976   1976.218

Name Inger-Lise + John Kilcoyne
Address 23A Woods Ave
Worc, Ma. 01606

Telephone 508 - 852 -1531

Name

Address

Telephone

Name

Address

Telephone

Name

Address

Telephone

Name

Address

Telephone

Name

Address

Telephone

Name

Address

Telephone

Name

Address

Telephone

Name

Address

Telephone

Name

Address

Telephone

Name

Address

Telephone

Name

Address

Telephone

Name

Address

Telephone

Name

Address

Telephone

Name

Address

Telephone

Name

Address

Telephone

Name

Address

Telephone

Name

Address

Telephone

Name

Address

Telephone

Name

Address

Telephone

Name

Address

Telephone

Name	Name
Address	Address
Telephone	Telephone
Name	Name
Address	Address
Telephone	Telephone
Name	Name
Address	Address
Telephone	Telephone
Name	Name
Address	Address
Telephone	Telephone
Name	Name
Address	Address
Telephone	Telephone

Name	Name
Address	Address
Telephone	Telephone
Name	Name
Address	Address
Telephone	Telephone
Name	Name
Address	Address
Telephone	Telephone
Name	Name
Address	Address
Telephone	Telephone
Name	Name
Address	Address
Telephone	Telephone

Beauty (Oiran)
Kitagawa Utamaro, Japanese, 1754–1806
Color woodblock print, 14^{15}/$_{16}$ × 9^{11}/$_{16}$ in., ca. 1800
H. O. Havemeyer Collection
Bequest of Mrs. H. O. Havemeyer, 1929   JP 1676

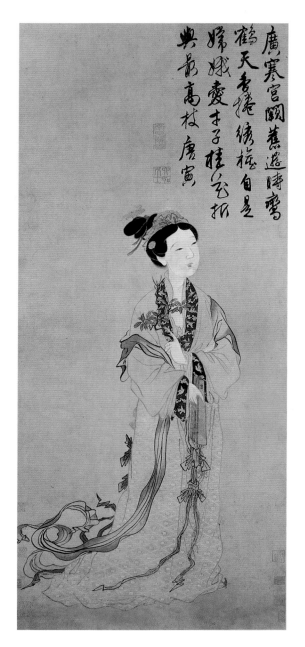

廣寒宮闕舊遊時鸞
鶴天香捲繡旗自是
嫦娥愛才子桂花分付
與最高枝 唐寅

The Moon Goddess Ch'ang O
T'ang Yin, Chinese, 1470–1524
Hanging scroll: ink and color on paper; 53½ × 23 in.
Gift of Douglas Dillon, 1981   1981.4.2

Name Danielle & Mark Lembo
Address 59 Windsor Ln
Marshfield 02050

Telephone

Name

Address

Telephone

Name

Address

Telephone

Name

Address

Telephone

Name

Address

Telephone

Name

Address

Telephone

Name

Address

Telephone

Name

Address

Telephone

Name

Address

Telephone

Name

Address

Telephone

Name	Name
Address	Address
Telephone	Telephone
Name	Name
Address	Address
Telephone	Telephone
Name	Name
Address	Address
Telephone	Telephone
Name	Name
Address	Address
Telephone	Telephone
Name	Name
Address	Address
Telephone	Telephone

Name

Address

Telephone

Name

Address

Telephone

Name

Address

Telephone

Name

Address

Telephone

Name

Address

Telephone

Name

Address

Telephone

Name

Address

Telephone

Name

Address

Telephone

Name

Address

Telephone

Name

Address

Telephone

Name	Name
Address	Address
Telephone	Telephone

Name	Name
Address	Address
Telephone	Telephone

Name	Name
Address	Address
Telephone	Telephone

Name	Name
Address	Address
Telephone	Telephone

Name	Name
Address	Address
Telephone	Telephone

M

Mademoiselle V. . . in the Costume of an Espada
Édouard Manet, French, 1832–1883
Oil on canvas, 65 × 50¼ in., 1862
H. O. Havemeyer Collection
Bequest of Mrs. H. O. Havemeyer, 1929   29.100.53

Bellona
Rembrandt van Rijn, Dutch, 1606–1669
Oil on canvas, 50 × 38⅜ in., 1633
The Friedsam Collection
Bequest of Michael Friedsam, 1931 32.100.23

Name Cathy + Bill Mahory
Address 19 Inverness Blvd
San Antonio, Texas 78230
210-492-8812
210-492-0911
Telephone Fax 210-492-5599

Cell - 210-867-5442

Name Maureen + Frank McGrath
Address 458 Kirby Dr.
Seabrook, Texas
77586

Telephone 281-326-6243

Name Bobby Martell
Address 153 Belmont St
Fall River, Ma. 02720

Cell 508-725-9578
Telephone 508-678-2799

Name Charlie Mooney
Address 15 Pheasand St
Unit 155
Harwich, Mass
Anchorage Condo #5524

Telephone

Name Eileen O'Meara
Address 36 Eliot St
Milton 02186

Telephone 617-698-5765

Cathy's friend
Name Gretchen Miranda
Address 15706 Spruce Stream St
San Antonio, Tx 78247

Telephone

Name
Address

Telephone

Name
Address

Telephone

Name
Address

Telephone

Name
Address

Telephone

Name

Address

Telephone

Name

Address

Telephone

Name

Address

Telephone

Name

Address

Telephone

Name

Address

Telephone

Name

Address

Telephone

Name

Address

Telephone

Name

Address

Telephone

Name

Address

Telephone

Name

Address

Telephone

Name	Name
Address	Address
Telephone	Telephone
Name	Name
Address	Address
Telephone	Telephone
Name	Name
Address	Address
Telephone	Telephone
Name	Name
Address	Address
Telephone	Telephone
Name	Name
Address	Address
Telephone	Telephone

Name

Address

Telephone

Name

Address

Telephone

Name

Address

Telephone

Name

Address

Telephone

Name

Address

Telephone

Name

Address

Telephone

Name

Address

Telephone

Name

Address

Telephone

Name

Address

Telephone

Name

Address

Telephone

Self-Portrait with Two Pupils,
Mademoiselle Marie Gabrielle Capet (1761–1818)
and Mademoiselle Carreaux de Rosemond (d. 1788)
Adélaïde Labille-Guiard, French, 1749–1803
Oil on canvas, 83 × 59½ in., 1785
Gift of Julia A. Berwind, 1953   53.225.5

N

Portrait of a Young Woman, Called
Mademoiselle Charlotte du Val d'Ognes
French, ca. 1800
Oil on canvas, 63½ × 50⅝ in.
Mr. and Mrs. Isaac D. Fletcher Collection
Bequest of Isaac D. Fletcher, 1917   17.120.204

Name Lois + Dave Nehl
Address 677 N. Green Dr.
Wheeling, Ill. 60090

Telephone 847-537-2223

Name
Address

Telephone

Name
Address

Telephone

Name
Address

Telephone

Name
Address

Telephone

Name
Address

Telephone

Name
Address

Telephone

Name
Address

Telephone

Name
Address

Telephone

Name
Address

Telephone

Name

Address

Telephone

Name

Address

Telephone

Name

Address

Telephone

Name

Address

Telephone

Name

Address

Telephone

Name

Address

Telephone

Name

Address

Telephone

Name

Address

Telephone

Name

Address

Telephone

Name

Address

Telephone

Name	Name
Address	Address
Telephone	Telephone
Name	Name
Address	Address
Telephone	Telephone
Name	Name
Address	Address
Telephone	Telephone
Name	Name
Address	Address
Telephone	Telephone
Name	Name
Address	Address
Telephone	Telephone

Name

Address

Telephone

Name

Address

Telephone

Name

Address

Telephone

Name

Address

Telephone

Name

Address

Telephone

Name

Address

Telephone

Name

Address

Telephone

Name

Address

Telephone

Name

Address

Telephone

Name

Address

Telephone

Princess and Attendants on a Balcony
Indian, Mughal period, 18th century
Album leaf: opaque watercolors and gold on paper,
13⅛ × 8¼ in.
Theodore M. Davis Collection
Bequest of Theodore M. Davis, 1915   30.95.174, folio 18

Two Tahitian Women
Paul Gauguin, French, 1848–1903
Oil on canvas, 37 × 28½ in., 1899
Gift of William Church Osborn, 1949   49.58.1

Name	Name
Address	Address
Telephone	Telephone
Name	Name
Address	Address
Telephone	Telephone
Name	Name
Address	Address
Telephone	Telephone
Name	Name
Address	Address
Telephone	Telephone
Name	Name
Address	Address
Telephone	Telephone

Name

Address

Telephone

Name

Address

Telephone

Name

Address

Telephone

Name

Address

Telephone

Name

Address

Telephone

Name

Address

Telephone

Name

Address

Telephone

Name

Address

Telephone

Name

Address

Telephone

Name

Address

Telephone

Name	Name
Address	Address
Telephone	Telephone

Name	Name
Address	Address
Telephone	Telephone

Name	Name
Address	Address
Telephone	Telephone

Name	Name
Address	Address
Telephone	Telephone

Name	Name
Address	Address
Telephone	Telephone

Name	Name
Address	Address
Telephone	Telephone
Name	Name
Address	Address
Telephone	Telephone
Name	Name
Address	Address
Telephone	Telephone
Name	Name
Address	Address
Telephone	Telephone
Name	Name
Address	Address
Telephone	Telephone

PQ

Portrait of the Artist
Mary Cassatt, American, 1844–1926
Gouache on paper, 23⅝ × 16³/₁₆ in., 1878
Bequest of Edith H. Proskauer, 1975   1975.319.1

PQ

Woman in White
Pablo Picasso, Spanish, 1881–1973
Oil on canvas, 39 × 31½ in., 1923
Rogers Fund, 1951; acquired from
The Museum of Modern Art,
Lillie P. Bliss Collection   53.140.4

Name	Name
Address	Address
Telephone	Telephone
Name	Name
Address	Address
Telephone	Telephone
Name	Name
Address	Address
Telephone	Telephone
Name	Name
Address	Address
Telephone	Telephone
Name	Name
Address	Address
Telephone	Telephone

Name	Name
Address	Address
Telephone	Telephone
Name	Name
Address	Address
Telephone	Telephone
Name	Name
Address	Address
Telephone	Telephone
Name	Name
Address	Address
Telephone	Telephone
Name	Name
Address	Address
Telephone	Telephone

Name	Name
Address	Address
Telephone	Telephone
Name	Name
Address	Address
Telephone	Telephone
Name	Name
Address	Address
Telephone	Telephone
Name	Name
Address	Address
Telephone	Telephone
Name	Name
Address	Address
Telephone	Telephone

Name

Address

Telephone

Name

Address

Telephone

Name

Address

Telephone

Name

Address

Telephone

Name

Address

Telephone

Name

Address

Telephone

Name

Address

Telephone

Name

Address

Telephone

Name

Address

Telephone

Name

Address

Telephone

R

Dish with the Bust of a Woman
Italian, Castel Durante, probably by the
"In Castel Durante" Painter
Ceramic, diam. 8½ in., ca. 1530
Robert Lehman Collection, 1975   1975.1.1084

R

Kylix (drinking cup)
Greek, Attic red-figure, attributed to the
Painter of Bologna 417
Terracotta (detail), entire diam. 14⅜ in.
ca. 460–450 B.C.
Rogers Fund, 1906   06.1021.167

Name	Name
Address	Address
Telephone	Telephone
Name	Name
Address	Address
Telephone	Telephone
Name	Name
Address	Address
Telephone	Telephone
Name	Name
Address	Address
Telephone	Telephone
Name	Name
Address	Address
Telephone	Telephone

Name	Name
Address	Address
Telephone	Telephone
Name	Name
Address	Address
Telephone	Telephone
Name	Name
Address	Address
Telephone	Telephone
Name	Name
Address	Address
Telephone	Telephone
Name	Name
Address	Address
Telephone	Telephone

Name	Name
Address	Address
Telephone	Telephone

Name	Name
Address	Address
Telephone	Telephone

Name	Name
Address	Address
Telephone	Telephone

Name	Name
Address	Address
Telephone	Telephone

Name	Name
Address	Address
Telephone	Telephone

Name

Address

Telephone

Name

Address

Telephone

Name

Address

Telephone

Name

Address

Telephone

Name

Address

Telephone

Name

Address

Telephone

Name

Address

Telephone

Name

Address

Telephone

Name

Address

Telephone

Name

Address

Telephone

S

The Love Letter
Jean Honoré Fragonard, French, 1732–1806
Oil on canvas, 32¾ × 26⅜ in.
The Jules Bache Collection, 1949   49.7.49

S

**Comtesse de la Châtre (Marie Charlotte Louise
Perrette Aglaé Bontemps, 1762–1848)**
Elisabeth Louise Vigée Le Brun, French, 1755–1842
Oil on canvas, 45 × 34½ in.
Gift of Jessie Woolworth Donahue, 1954   54.182

Name	Name
Address	Address
Telephone	Telephone
Name	Name
Address	Address
Telephone	Telephone
Name	Name
Address	Address
Telephone	Telephone
Name	Name
Address	Address
Telephone	Telephone
Name	Name
Address	Address
Telephone	Telephone

Name	Name
Address	Address
Telephone	Telephone

Name	Name
Address	Address
Telephone	Telephone

Name	Name
Address	Address
Telephone	Telephone

Name	Name
Address	Address
Telephone	Telephone

Name	Name
Address	Address
Telephone	Telephone

Name	Name
Address	Address
Telephone	Telephone
Name	Name
Address	Address
Telephone	Telephone
Name	Name
Address	Address
Telephone	Telephone
Name	Name
Address	Address
Telephone	Telephone
Name	Name
Address	Address
Telephone	Telephone

Name	Name
Address	Address
Telephone	Telephone

Name	Name
Address	Address
Telephone	Telephone

Name	Name
Address	Address
Telephone	Telephone

Name	Name
Address	Address
Telephone	Telephone

Name	Name
Address	Address
Telephone	Telephone

T

L'Espagnole: Harmonie en Bleu
Henri Matisse, French, 1869–1954
Oil on canvas, 18½ × 14 in.
Robert Lehman Collection, 1975   1975.1.193

T

Jeanne Hébuterne
Amedeo Modigliani, Italian, 1884–1920
Oil on canvas, 36 × 28¾ in., 1918
Gift of Mr. and Mrs. Nate B. Spingold, 1956   56.184.2

Name	Name
Address	Address
Telephone	Telephone
Name	Name
Address	Address
Telephone	Telephone
Name	Name
Address	Address
Telephone	Telephone
Name	Name
Address	Address
Telephone	Telephone
Name	Name
Address	Address
Telephone	Telephone

Name		Name	
Address		Address	
Telephone		Telephone	
Name		Name	
Address		Address	
Telephone		Telephone	
Name		Name	
Address		Address	
Telephone		Telephone	
Name		Name	
Address		Address	
Telephone		Telephone	
Name		Name	
Address		Address	
Telephone		Telephone	

Name

Address

Telephone

Name

Address

Telephone

Name

Address

Telephone

Name

Address

Telephone

Name

Address

Telephone

Name

Address

Telephone

Name

Address

Telephone

Name

Address

Telephone

Name

Address

Telephone

Name

Address

Telephone

Name

Address

Telephone

Name

Address

Telephone

Name

Address

Telephone

Name

Address

Telephone

Name

Address

Telephone

Name

Address

Telephone

Name

Address

Telephone

Name

Address

Telephone

Name

Address

Telephone

Name

Address

Telephone

Lady with Her Pets (Molly Wales Fobes)
Rufus Hathaway, American, 1770–1822
Oil on canvas, 34¼ × 32 in., 1790
Gift of Edgar William and Bernice Chrysler Garbisch, 1963   63.201.1

UV

UV

Mrs. John Winthrop
John Singleton Copley, American, 1738–1815
Oil on canvas, 35½ × 28¾ in., 1773
Morris K. Jesup Fund, 1931   31.109

Name	Name
Address	Address
Telephone	Telephone

Name	Name
Address	Address
Telephone	Telephone

Name	Name
Address	Address
Telephone	Telephone

Name	Name
Address	Address
Telephone	Telephone

Name	Name
Address	Address
Telephone	Telephone

Name	Name
Address	Address
Telephone	Telephone
Name	Name
Address	Address
Telephone	Telephone
Name	Name
Address	Address
Telephone	Telephone
Name	Name
Address	Address
Telephone	Telephone
Name	Name
Address	Address
Telephone	Telephone

Name

Address

Telephone

Name

Address

Telephone

Name

Address

Telephone

Name

Address

Telephone

Name

Address

Telephone

Name

Address

Telephone

Name

Address

Telephone

Name

Address

Telephone

Name

Address

Telephone

Name

Address

Telephone

Name	Name
Address	Address
Telephone	Telephone
Name	Name
Address	Address
Telephone	Telephone
Name	Name
Address	Address
Telephone	Telephone
Name	Name
Address	Address
Telephone	Telephone
Name	Name
Address	Address
Telephone	Telephone

Woman Playing a Kithara (detail)
Fresco from the Villa of
P. Fannius Synistor at Boscoreale
Roman, 40–30 B.C.
Entire fresco 6 ft. 1½ in. × 6 ft. 1½ in.
Rogers Fund, 1903   03.14.5

W

Portrait of a Woman
Egyptian, from Fayum, Roman Period, ca. A.D. 138–161
Encaustic on wood, h. 15 in.
Rogers Fund, 1909   09.181.6

W

Name	Name
Address	Address
Telephone	Telephone

Name	Name
Address	Address
Telephone	Telephone

Name	Name
Address	Address
Telephone	Telephone

Name	Name
Address	Address
Telephone	Telephone

Name	Name
Address	Address
Telephone	Telephone

Name	Name
Address	Address
Telephone	Telephone
Name	Name
Address	Address
Telephone	Telephone
Name	Name
Address	Address
Telephone	Telephone
Name	Name
Address	Address
Telephone	Telephone
Name	Name
Address	Address
Telephone	Telephone

Name

Address

Telephone

Name

Address

Telephone

Name

Address

Telephone

Name

Address

Telephone

Name

Address

Telephone

Name

Address

Telephone

Name

Address

Telephone

Name

Address

Telephone

Name

Address

Telephone

Name

Address

Telephone

Name	Name
Address	Address
Telephone	Telephone

Name	Name
Address	Address
Telephone	Telephone

Name	Name
Address	Address
Telephone	Telephone

Name	Name
Address	Address
Telephone	Telephone

Name	Name
Address	Address
Telephone	Telephone

By the Seashore
Pierre-Auguste Renoir, French, 1841–1919
Oil on canvas, 31¼ × 28½ in., 1883
H. O. Havemeyer Collection
Bequest of Mrs. H. O. Havemeyer, 1929   29.100.125

XY
Z

The Singer in Green
Edgar Degas, French, 1834–1917
Pastel on light blue laid paper, 23¾ × 18¼ in.
Bequest of Stephen C. Clark, 1960   61.107.7

XY
Z

Name	Name
Address	Address
Telephone	Telephone
Name	Name
Address	Address
Telephone	Telephone
Name	Name
Address	Address
Telephone	Telephone
Name	Name
Address	Address
Telephone	Telephone
Name	Name
Address	Address
Telephone	Telephone

Name	Name
Address	Address
Telephone	Telephone

Name	Name
Address	Address
Telephone	Telephone

Name	Name
Address	Address
Telephone	Telephone

Name	Name
Address	Address
Telephone	Telephone

Name	Name
Address	Address
Telephone	Telephone

Name

Address

Telephone

Name

Address

Telephone

Name

Address

Telephone

Name

Address

Telephone

Name

Address

Telephone

Name

Address

Telephone

Name

Address

Telephone

Name

Address

Telephone

Name

Address

Telephone

Name

Address

Telephone

Name

Address

Telephone

Name

Address

Telephone

Name

Address

Telephone

Name

Address

Telephone

Name

Address

Telephone

Name

Address

Telephone

Name

Address

Telephone

Name

Address

Telephone

Name

Address

Telephone

Name

Address

Telephone